the sky is black and blue like a battered child
by
Ben Arzate

Dedicated to Darrell and Marge Jurmu

Acknowledgments

"brad" was published in *Sketch*, Vol 73.

"the sky is black and blue like a battered child" and "bone dust and glitter" were published in *Radical Dislocations: Best New Underground Poets* from Chupa Cabra House.

"the sky is black and blue like a battered child," "shower," and "shower, again" were published on *TwentySomething Press* (twentysomethingpress.tumblr.com).

Special thanks to Garrett Cook for editing the first draft.

The dance becomes wilder and wilder. Laughter from the coffin.
On a swing a Madonna with breast cancer. Horatio opens an
umbrella, embraces Hamlet. Freeze in the embrace under the
umbrella. The breast cancer shines like a sun.

- Heiner Muller, *Hamletmachine*

Then we saw her.
She was hanging there, swaying, with twisted cords
roped round her neck. When Oedipus saw her,
with a dreadful groan he took her body
from the noose in which she hung, and then,
when the poor woman was lying on the ground—
what happened next was a horrific sight—
from her clothes he ripped the golden brooches
she wore as ornaments, raised them high,
and drove them deep into his eyeballs,
crying as he did so: "You will no longer see
all those atrocious things I suffered,
the dreadful things I did! No. You have seen
what you never should have looked upon,
and what I wished to know you did not see.
So now and for all future time be dark!"

- Sophocles, *Oedipus the King*

The passion for destruction is a creative passion, too.

- Mikhail Bakunin, *The Reaction in Germany*

orgy haiku

answer this for me
what if they gave an orgy
and nobody came?

bone dust and glitter

i woke in a bath of syringes and broken glass
a harpy perched upon my chest.
the ghosts that float around my
in-the-clouds head had abandoned me
to a state of mental ne'er-do-well.
babies screamed for a mother's touch and food
that they'd never have again.
buildings burned as they had
since the time of the great white nothing
and the poison air was thinner
while blades were left unsated.

i wanted to tell you how much i love you
but the urge to peel back your flesh
and embrace your smooth skeleton was far too strong.
as i lay next to you,
i watch the lights dance behind my eyelids.
they remind me of when meaning meant something
and hatred was not just boredom.

no sense intended to be made.

i've been asleep inside a box full of comfortable lies
and packing peanuts for the past two weeks.
it's time to wake up.

the milk has gone sour, the bread has gone stale and my chance to apologize has passed

i want to bang my head against the wall
until it cracks
then i will listen to my thoughts
leak out of the crack like music and static
from a broken radio

i want to live in a secluded cabin in the woods
with a laptop with a satellite internet connection
and start a twitter
where i do nothing but complain about how lonely i am

i will take a stringless guitar to an open mic
and i will stand on the stage with it
i will breath heavily into the microphone
and glare at the audience
until someone asks me to leave

i will download a porn video off the internet
and i will print off every frame
and make a flip book
i will make several and then sell them
to elementary school boys

last saturday i bought an expensive suit
wore it out of the store
then i spent all day riding the bus

on the last bus of the day
i got off at the house of someone i never met
i slipped a note under the door that said
'hey, that thing last night? sorry about that'
then i walked home.

human skin lampshade

an empty studio apartment
there is a lamp and a rotary telephone on the hardwood floor
a young woman enters and closes and locks the door behind
her
she sits cross-legged on the floor
between the lamp and the telephone
she reaches under the human skin lampshade
and turns on the light
the telephone rings and the girl answers
hello, she says
yes, yes
please call back in an hour, she says
she hangs up
there is a pounding noise outside the window
the young woman brings her knees up to her chest
she wraps her arms around her legs and stares at the floor
in the window, a man's head with no mouth, no nostrils
and unnaturally huge eyes rises up
it stares at the young woman
it breathes heavily despite the absence of airholes
do not acknowledge it, do not acknowledge it
the young woman repeats to herself
the phone rings again
she picks up, keeping her eyes to the floor
yes, yes, i understand, i'll keep waiting here
she hangs up
the head in the window continues to stare and breathe
how i wish he'd just go away
the young woman thinks

brad

i started getting calls
a month ago

they were all the same woman
asking for brad

they were all
the same wrong number

they finally stopped
and my phone hasn't rung
for almost three weeks

i miss those calls

untitled

i'm going to take all the stuff you gave me
including that bag
i will put all the stuff in the bag
i will take the bag to your door
and hang it on the doorknob
i will look at the decorations on your door
and i will feel so small
then i will turn around and go home

the sky is black and blue like a battered child

all hopes and dreams had been destroyed in a meth lab
explosion
pieces of a dead cat were scattered all over the street
a rusty, beat up truck with a flat tire drove by
its rim scrapping against the street and sending up sparks

the sky is black and blue like a battered child
the air is thick enough
that you could press someone's face against it
and suffocate them to death

i run under a tree and stand with my back against the trunk
until the rain stops
an obese old man walks by me and smiles
he has only three black teeth and smells like a hospital

during this scene, the camera pans back to behind the camera
to reveal that the cameraman has gone on break
or, more likely, was never there at all

i walk home across pavement
that the traffic lights go into like dripping paint
junk mail in my mailbox and inbox
remind me that (for better or for worse)
i'm still on the grid
and i write this to remind you
that if you are aware of these words at all
you probably are too

i jerked off to error messages on my computer
then watched tv static to calm my nerves
though i have little i actually
need to be nervous about

your face and mine

i want to tear your face off
and nail it to mine

i will have the inner part face out
and your skin pressed to mine

my face will look inside out
and i will always have your lips against mine

safety pin

today i was chewing
on a safety pin

the pin came open
between my lips

it pricked my upper lip
then fell out of my mouth

a drop of blood from my lip
followed it to the floor

a void opened in the carpet
closing before the blood
could follow the safety pin through

i looked at the drop of blood
on the carpet and felt sad

i hate when old people complain

i hate when old people
complain about their back pains
i hate when old people
complain about their arthritis

i hate when old people
complain about how they can't do anything
but sleep and watch tv all day

i hate when old people complain
because their complaints always remind me
that they will be gone soon

five haiku

a haiku about sickness

i just called in sick
i wasn't lying, i feel
how i always feel

a haiku about fatigue

i woke up at two
in the afternoon today
then went back to sleep

a haiku about uncertainty

'what's in store for me?'
when i try to ponder this
i have crying jags

a haiku about defeat

'oh fuck it', i say
i have been saying that phrase
more often lately

a haiku about regret

i now hate all these
haiku, but i hate all things
i do at some point

reflection text

distorted, elongated images of traffic lights in wet pavement like paint dripping into a black canvas
a truck with a flat tire drives by
sparks reflected in the nearby puddle where they are extinguished
street lights in a dark window like a picture of the night sky
a husband and wife lay in bed
their bodies melt and flow into the headboard
the fluid turns silver and becomes a mirror
daylight shines off the headboard mirror
a man walks in the room
he looks around
he walks up to the bed
he takes a gun a sitting on the headboard
we walks into another door on the other side of the room
he stands in the bathroom and looks in the mirror
he sticks the gun in his mouth and pulls the trigger
blood and pieces of brain and skull spray the tile wall behind him
his reflection stands there with an empty hand against his chin
he opens the bathroom door
there is a black void
he walks towards into the void until he appears a white spot
more white spots appear in the black void
street lights in a dark window like a picture of the night sky

alfred jarry is dead

have you ever woken up with a deep sense of dread
because the only thing you could remember from your dream
is that your bike had a flat tire?

alley

i will crouch in the alley
and wait for you to walk by
when you do
i will pull you into the alley
and rape you
but it will not be an actual rape
it will be an elaborate roleplay
we worked out beforehand
we will not be seen in the alley
but we will be excited by the possibility
when we are both spent
we will lay on the floor of the alley
and you will be beautiful
among the garbage and debris
then we will go home
we will take a shower together
sit on the bed
and watch leni riefenstahl films

good night day dreams

every night at 7:30
your son watches dead air for an hour
he says it's his favorite show

your smile is a piss-stained grate

i knew a guitarist
who shredded his fingers on
the strings while playing a show
he proudly displays the blood-stained guitar
in his living room

the radio plays mozart
the tv plays static
while she sits on her bed
and reads *flowers in the attic*

moral of the story:
you can't yell at the crackheads of the world
there are more of them than there are of you

my heart is a molding strawberry

one morning, i woke up in the middle of the night
it was bright and sunny and heavy rain was pouring
it was so hot, i thought I would freeze to death

i'm boxing with the wall
and the wall is winning

the toilet is clogged with pubic hair
someone else's pubic hair

i could use the plunger on it
but i think i'll just stare into space
until i see colors inverted

untitled

you know those people
who are sober right now
and are totally ok with that?

those people suck

when my boat has sunk

when my boat has sunk
and all of it is submerged
encased in deep green
and any of my belongings not trapped inside
are washed out to shore
for children building sandcastles to find
and all my letters to you
have blurred into nonsense and dissolved
and my flailing body
has finally given in and drowned
and has been picked clean by the fish
and all the wood has rotted
and all the metal has rusted
at the bottom
nothing will be visible from the surface
especially from your plane
which will pass over
in the briefest possible moment

shower

i was taking a shower in my college dorm
i was mumbling various things to myself
i got out and dried off
i went to the sinks to brush my teeth and comb my hair
there was someone standing at the sinks

who were you talking to, he said
i was just talking to myself, i said
are you sure, he said
about what, he said
nothing really, i said
are you ok, he said
i'm not crazy if that's what you mean, i said
sometimes there are things that talk to us that aren't us, he said
like what, i said
like spirits, he said
okay, i said
you don't want any of them talking to you, he said
i wasn't talking to any ghosts, i said
okay, he said

then he left

shower, again

i took a shower this morning
when i got out, i found that the world had ended
i guess that shower was pretty pointless

About the Author

Ben Arzate lives in Des Moines, IA.
This is his first poetry collection.
He blogs at dripdropdripdropdripdrop.blogspot.com
and can be contacted at benarz13@gmail.com.

Printed in Great Britain
by Amazon

17517004R00020